Original title:
Songs of the Sparkling Tree

Copyright © 2024 Creative Arts Management OÜ
All rights reserved.

Author: Clara Whitfield
ISBN HARDBACK: 978-9916-94-376-2
ISBN PAPERBACK: 978-9916-94-377-9

Anthems from the Celestial Canopy

Up in the branches, the critters convene,
Squirrels wear hats, oh what a scene!
Chirping the tunes from the tops of their heads,
Dancing on leaves, like they're all well-fed.

The owl's got rhythm, it's quite the display,
Hooting a jig, come join in the fray!
Bunnies are bouncing with glee all around,
They hop to the beat of the forest's own sound.

Frogs in tuxedos, with tails that are long,
Croak in the chorus, it's a wacky song!
The wind starts to shuffle, a whimsical breeze,
As everyone shimmies, they all aim to please.

Beneath the bright moon, a party takes flight,
The critters are twirling through the deep, starry night.
Laughter and gasps fill the evening so clear,
In their own little world, with naught but good cheer.

Refrains from the Twilit Arbor

In the branches, monkeys swing,
Chasing dreams with bladder-swing.
Squirrels dance on tightrope lines,
Nutty antics, oh how it shines!

Hooting owls join the fun,
Telling tales 'til setting sun.
Breezes whisper, leaves all laugh,
Nature's joy in a splendid half.

Tones of the Gleaming Trees

Bugs in tuxedos tap their feet,
Dancing circles, quite the feat.
Fireflies flash their disco light,
Oh, what a twinkling, sparkling sight!

Chirping frogs hold the best show,
With a croak and a leap, they go.
Under the stars, they form a band,
Ribbits echo, quite unplanned!

Odes to the Sparkling Canopy

Raccoons in masks sneak and peek,
Planning mischief, cheek to cheek.
While the moon winks from above,
They share secrets, laugh in love.

A turtle slow, but wise beyond,
Sips the dew and feasts on fronds.
With every drip, a chirpy cheer,
Glowing tales fill the night air here.

Verses in the Illuminated Thicket

Giggling leaves tickle the breeze,
Caterpillars shine with ease.
Chasing shadows, they play tag,
In this forest, joy won't lag.

A dapper fox in spectacles,
Reads the trees like manuals.
With a chuckle, he shows the way,
To grand adventures that won't sway!

Serenade of the Radiant Orchard

In a grove where giggles bloom,
Fruits wear hats, dispelling gloom.
A squirrel juggles nuts on high,
While the rabbits try to fly.

Cherries dance on tiny feet,
Making every picnic sweet.
Lemonade flows from the trees,
Tickling fancy with the breeze.

Harmonies from the Dazzling Branches

A parrot sings a funny tune,
Underneath the bright, round moon.
In the shade, the shadows prance,
As the owls join in the dance.

Quirky leaves sway left and right,
Tickling grass in morning light.
Pickles bounce from branch to branch,
Inviting all to join the chant.

Ballads of the Luminescent Woods

In the woods where lanterns giggle,
Bouncing bugs make everyone wiggle.
A raccoon plays a tune on drums,
While the wind merrily hums.

Glowing mushrooms tell tall tales,
Of dancing frogs and silly snails.
Every critter joins the show,
Wiggly worms put on a glow.

Chants of the Brilliant Foliage

In the tree tops, laughter swells,
As the gummy bears cast their spells.
A bumblebee wears a bright tie,
Winking as it buzzes by.

Maple syrup oceans flow,
Sugarplum trees all lined in a row.
Frothy clouds bounce in the sky,
With giggles echoing nearby.

Echoing Dreams of the Twilight Grove

In the hush of night, a frog starts to croak,
A squirrel joins in, with a nut for a joke.
Fireflies flicker, like children at play,
While beetles in bow ties dance night away.

The trees, they giggle, their branches twist tight,
As owls wear spectacles, reading by light.
Whispers of rustling, the critters all chat,
A hedgehog declares, 'I prefer a top hat!'

A Celebration of Luminescence and Life

The moonlight chuckles, it's dressed in a veil,
While mushrooms in hats tell a wacky tale.
Crickets are tap dancing, showing their moves,
While the raccoons practice their fancy grooves.

The breeze carries laughter, so light and so sweet,
As a rabbit in glasses takes a bow with his feet.
Daisies are clapping, their petals in cheer,
As a bear plays the flute, spreading joy far and near.

Crescendos Among the Glittering Treetops

The stars play maracas, jangling so bright,
While chipmunks juggle acorns, what a sight!
A porcupine croons, with a voice like a bell,
As a wise old tortoise joins in with a yell.

The branches all sway to their own silly tune,
As squirrels declare, 'We shall dance till it's noon!'
The laughter echoes, like bubbles of air,
In this woodland concert, there's joy everywhere.

The Dance of Dappled Light

A lizard in slippers does the cha-cha,
While butterflies joke, 'Catch me if you can!'
The foliage sways, with glee in their frames,
As the wind starts to whistle some silly refrains.

The shadows all chuckle, mixing in play,
Each leaf tells a story, in its own funny way.
A family of owls, roosted up high,
Gathers for storytime, under the sky.

Serenade of the Brilliant Blossoms

In the garden of giggles, blooms start to dance,
A daisy in a top hat, taking a chance.
The roses tell jokes, oh what a sight,
While tulips do cartwheels, hearts feeling light.

Chirping with laughter, butterflies glide,
Their wings fluttering, a colorful ride.
Bees buzz a chorus, with unkempt hair,
As the blossoms all chuckle in the spring air.

Sounds from the Resplendent Hedge

Hedges whisper secrets, quite full of glee,
A squirrel in a tie, sipping some tea.
The hedgehogs play poker, with acorns galore,
While rabbits debate who's the fastest (for sure).

With each rustling leaf, a chorus erupts,
The hedges are laughing, but who interrupts?
A snail in a bowler hat, moving so slow,
Calls out to the crowd, 'Let's put on a show!'

Harmonies Through the Shimmering Leaves

Leaves clink like glasses, in sync with the breeze,
A caterpillar waltzes, with such graceful ease.
An owl in a monocle sings out a tune,
While the crickets snap fingers, under the moon.

Choruses bubble from branches so bright,
Acorns drop down, they've found their delight.
With every odd note, the trees start to sway,
And laughter erupts, as night turns to day.

Verses of the Illuminous Thicket

In a thicket so bright, where the mushrooms glow,
Frogs wear funny hats, putting on a show.
Fireflies flicker, like they're lost in a dance,
While the raccoons debate, 'Who took my last glance?'

Laughter erupts, as the shadows all play,
While hedgehogs recite jokes, brightening the day.
Each twig and each fern chimes in with a cheer,
In this thicket of humor, there's nothing to fear.

Whispers of the Shimmering Canopy

Underneath the leafy chat,
Squirrels dance with a silly hat.
Birds in pairs sing off-key tunes,
While everyone else just laughs and swoons.

Branches sway in laughter's glee,
A wise old owl hoots, 'Come see!'
Raccoons jive, a clumsy stance,
Nature's party, all take a chance.

In the shade, the shadows prance,
Critters join in a silly dance.
Frogs leap high, mischief ablaze,
While crickets tease in a buzzing haze.

Under stars, they swap tall tales,
Of winding roots and breezy gales.
The canopy whispers their delight,
As laughter echoes into the night.

Melodies of the Twinkling Boughs

Up in the branches, sounds collide,
A squirrel's squeak, a crow's caw ride.
Jays wear wigs made of mossy green,
While chipmunks put on a show so keen.

The breezes giggle, tickling leaves,
As nature's jokers spin their weaves.
Pinecones roll down a sloped embank,
With everyone laughing, that's what they thank.

Frogs on lily pads sway and grin,
Telling stories of who might win.
A rabbit lost in its own big dream,
Dances along with a silly theme.

The night falls, stars twinkle bright,
Furry friends bask in the light.
They hum sweet tunes of joy and cheer,
In their world, every laugh is dear.

Lullabies Beneath the Glimmering Leaves

Beneath the glow of moonlit beams,
Foxes giggle and plot their schemes.
Bunnies bumble in playful stealth,
Sharing secrets of laughter and health.

Crickets play their tiny guitars,
While fireflies shine like little stars.
Each leaf a stage for stories grand,
Where everyone's given a funny hand.

Flip-flopped toads in a hopping race,
With silly faces, they pick their pace.
Twirling and whirling, round and around,
Every croak is a melody found.

In the hush of night, they drift to sleep,
But giggles linger, sweet and deep.
Dreams of mischief among the trees,
Singing softly with the warm, soft breeze.

Echoes in the Glittering Grove

In a grove where sparkles tease,
A frog wears boots, just to please.
Chattering birds share silly puns,
While daisies dance and make a fuss.

The rustling leaves join in the fun,
Breezes carry each burst of pun.
A hedgehog spins with leaves like twirl,
While owls giggle and give a whirl.

Down the paths where giggles swell,
The ants tell tales of their great spell.
Each tiny creature with a role,
Together share one joyful whole.

And as the day fades, laughter flies,
Under twilight's shimmery skies.
In the grove where joy runs free,
Life's a joke for you and me.

Songs of the Glowing Woodlands

In a forest where squirrels wear hats,
And dance with the frisky acrobats,
The mushrooms debate about the game,
While fireflies flicker, calling your name.

The owls have a stand-up routine,
They joke about scenes they have seen,
While chipmunks critique the night air,
And laugh till their cheeks turn a flare.

The bunnies organize a parade,
In costumes that shine, unafraid,
With carrots in hand, they strut wide,
In this woodland where giggles abide.

A raccoon sings high in a tree,
With a voice that sounds quite like a bee,
His friends in the shadows just grin,
Hoping he'll finish, so they can begin.

Nocturnes Under the Glittering Leaves

Under silver leaves, frogs sing in style,
With tunes that can stretch for a mile,
The crickets tap dance in the dark,
While shadows move with a magical spark.

The owls hoot riddles above the ground,
While squirrels spin stories, profound,
A fox plays the flute, quite offbeat,
As the night critters shuffle their feet.

A chorus of laughter spills through the air,
As fireflies giggle without a care,
The glow worms throw a disco ball,
And everyone joins in, one and all.

With each silly note, the forest shakes,
As even the shyest of creatures awakes,
To sing and to sway 'neath the gleaming sky,
In nocturnal delight, they all fly high!

The Celestial Choir of the Forest

In the still of the night, a symphony starts,
With raccoons playing homemade guitars,
While squirrels in tuxedos take the stage,
Flipping their tails with atmospheric rage.

The hedgehogs beat drums made of leaves,
As the fox sings tunes that no one believes,
A trombone's made from a hollowed-out log,
As frogs join in with a ribbiting clog.

Starlight sparkles like glittering rocks,
As the forest fidgets, laughing in flocks,
The trees sway along to this bizarre beat,
With branches that pulse to the rhythm of feet.

Outrageous the sounds from this woodland choir,
As up in the branches, their antics transpire,
A cacophony perfect for joyous delight,
As the creatures all dance, under soft moonlight.

Melodic Whispers of the Sunlit Branches

In sunlight's embrace, the birds get their cue,
To belt out a tune that's fresh as the dew,
While a beaver conducts with flair so divine,
A wooden stick seems to blow their mind.

The butterflies float like dancers in flight,
Twisting and turning, creating pure light,
A squirrel takes selfies, his grin is so wide,
As he captures his friends who are caught in a tide.

Giggling branches echo a cheerful laugh,
Mice join in with a silly autograph,
Each leaf is a note, each twig is a beat,
Creating a jive that is oh so sweet.

With joy in the air, the breeze starts to sway,
Bringing laughter and cheer to the forest each day,
A marvelous concert, full of pure glee,
In the wonderful world of whimsy, you see.

Dreamy Echoes Beneath the Verdant Arbors

Under the leaves, whispers collide,
Squirrels wear ties, with acorns as pride.
Dancing in circles, branches do sway,
Trees gossip loudly about yesterday.

A frog plays a tune on a flute made of grass,
While worms in tuxedos rumble and pass.
Mice are in choir, with cheese on their notes,
Balloons tied to branches, they all sing and gloat.

The sun cracks a joke, while shadows all laugh,
Even the shadows are taking a bath!
A breeze steals the hats from the birds up above,
Trimming the treetops with soft, gentle love.

Nuts fall like confetti, a party in bloom,
With each little rattle, there's music, a boom.
The laughter of branches fills up the blue air,
Welcome to jesting beneath foliage rare.

Celestial Chants in the Foliage

Stars sneak a peek through the leafy embrace,
Whispering secrets, while crickets keep pace.
A comet zooms in, flips pancakes on trees,
Singing of biscuits, just acting with ease.

Moonbeams are making some jellies tonight,
While owls roast marshmallows, taking delight.
The branches all sway to the tunes of the skies,
All creatures agree, it's a sudden surprise.

Chirps turn to giggles as rabbits break dance,
Rotating in circles, they take every chance.
In this cosmic party, no worries or fears,
Our laughter's the spark that ignites all the cheers.

With twinkling stars as our disco ball bright,
The forest keeps rocking till morning's first light.
What a funny gathering, a spectacle pure,
In nature's own theater, where joy is the cure.

With a Radiant Heart Among the Trees

With a radiant heart, I skipped through the grove,
Where leaves threw confetti and sunshine did strove.
A bear told a joke—got punched in the gut,
As rabbits fell over, in fits, they all shut.

Chipmunks made smoothies with berries in tow,
With frenzied excitement, their laughter would flow.
They twirled and they swirled, wearing hats made of twine,
Together they played, oh, what a fun line!

The flowers bring gossip, all dressed in bright hues,
While bees buzz around, sipping sweet morning dew.
Nature's own concert is lively and sweet,
With every small creature tapping toddler-like feet.

Under the sunlight, joy's echo so loud,
A waltz of enchantment, we sing for the crowd.
With hearts ever radiant, we dance in delight,
In this vibrant embrace, all worries take flight.

Musings in the Sparkling Wilderness

In the wilderness bright, where giggles abound,
A raccoon with glasses is spinning around.
He's teaching a lesson on eating with flair,
While ducks in canoes are racing through air.

The reeds start to chatter, exchanging bright tales,
Of turtles in derby hats chasing big snails.
Yet laughter erupts from a bumblebee choir,
Singing of nectar, a sweet, buzzing fire.

Trees shimmy and shake, with a rhythm unique,
While loons play charades, oh, what a mystique!
A parade of odd critters, all ready to cheer,
With confetti-stuffed pockets, they all draw near.

A snail lost his map, but he's not in despair,
He glides with a grin, full of joy in his glare.
With freedom and fun, every moment's a song,
In this sparkling wilderness, where we all belong.

Nature's Serenade Among the Sparkling Leaves

In the morning light, the squirrels dance,
They twirl and spin, giving leaves a chance.
The birds sing off-key, a feathery choir,
While ants march by in a line, like a wire.

The flowers giggle, pollen in their glee,
As frogs croak jokes, a funny spree.
A butterfly flits with a wink and a nod,
While bees buzz softly, looking quite odd.

The breeze plays tag, swirling all around,
Chasing the shadows that leap on the ground.
A raccoon rolls by, with a comedic flail,
As the trees chuckle at this funny tale.

Nature's laughter echoes, a joke in the air,
With every rustle, a punchline laid bare.
It's a symphony of smiles in pure jubilation,
Where the wit of the wild fuels cheerful elation.

Echoes of the Blessed Canopy

The leaves are gossiping, oh what a scene,
They share the secrets of what they have seen.
A squirrel in spandex gives quite a show,
As a chipmunk laughs, 'Is that fashion or woe?'

Clouds drift by, wearing hats quite absurd,
One hovers low, calling softly, unheard.
The wind rolls through, with a ticklish tease,
Rustling the branches, making them sneeze.

The berries blush, each round and sweet,
As a wren struts by on its tiny little feet.
A garden of giggles, where laughter is free,
In the echoes that bounce from the blessed canopy.

The sun plays peek-a-boo, a radiant jest,
Painting the leaves in its golden dress.
Here, joy trees blossom in whimsical cheer,
In this playful quilt where we draw near.

Poetics of the Lustrous Trees

Amidst the trunks, where shadows rule,
The owls tell tales that humorously fool.
A beaver grins, with his teeth so wide,
While the raccoon winks and tries to hide.

The pine cones giggle, full of delight,
As chipmunks scury, with antics in flight.
The trees sway gently, dancing with glee,
Whispering verses of pure jubilee.

In this lush theater, the crickets rehearse,
A comedy act that flows through the verse.
The ferns join in with a flourish so grand,
While mushrooms chuckle, all part of the band.

Under the moon, a party takes flight,
When fireflies join to spell out goodnight.
The stars shine bright, with a twinkle so bold,
As the poetics of laughter and nature unfold.

Songs Beneath the Starry Canopy

Beneath the stars, a raccoon sings,
With a voice so strange, it gives joy to things.
The owls hoot back, in a playful debate,
While insects tap dance, keeping up with the fate.

A drumming woodpecker starts a big beat,
With critters joining, all tapping their feet.
The moon winks in, as if in on the joke,
Adding a glow, a light-hearted poke.

The wildflowers sway, in a rhythmic trance,
Chasing fireflies, in a twinkly dance.
A hedgehog jives, with its spiky suit,
As everyone giggles, in this nightly pursuit.

With every chuckle, a new tale is spun,
Of squirrels and leaves, under shadows they run.
Here, laughter ascends like a song on the breeze,
Beneath the vast canvas of twinkling trees.

Overtures of the Brilliant Greenery

High above the boughs sway,
Squirrels dance in bright ballet.
Nuts are thrown with cheeky flair,
Everyone's included there.

Leaves whisper secrets, oh so sly,
Daring birds to swoop and fly.
Crickets chirp a cheeky tune,
Under the watch of the bright moon.

A rabbit hops, a turtle spins,
A merry chase, let the fun begin.
With laughter echoing through the trails,
Nature's humor never fails.

Even the ants join in the chase,
Somersaults in a crowded space.
As pinecones fall like confetti rain,
Nature's party is quite insane!

Melodies of the Golden Canopy

Sunshine filters through the leaves,
Caterpillars wear tiny sleeves.
Bouncing bugs and buzzing bees,
Share their wits with joyful ease.

A squirrel with a hat so grand,
Juggles acorns – isn't he planned?
While rabbits hop and kick up dust,
In this leafy realm, we trust.

The wind adds a playful sigh,
Poking fun at passersby.
Fluffy clouds roll high above,
Rainbows here, like a joke of love.

Branches sway, a quirky beat,
Nature's dance that can't be beat.
With every rustle, giggles start,
Laughter spreads—it's nature's art!

Echoes from the Emerald Canopy

Among the branches, echo bright,
Parrots mimic in morning light.
Lizards lounge, quite laid-back,
Listening to the bold geese quack.

A fox in shades, what a sight,
Strutting through the woods, so light.
With one paw up, he breaks the rules,
A master of the woodland schools.

Overhanging vines tease their friends,
Swinging gently, the laughter never ends.
A toad croaks out an off-key song,
While the others chime in, singing along.

Each tree stands tall, a wise old sage,
Sharing stories of every page.
In laughter and jest, all unite,
In the emerald world, pure delight!

Jigs of the Glittering Grove

In the grove, the party starts,
With twirling leaves and flapping hearts.
Mice put on their tiny shoes,
Ready to boogie, sing and cruise.

Branches sway like dancing fools,
Carrying whispers of nature's rules.
An owl hoots with a knowing grin,
As little critters begin to spin.

Snakes slide by with a smooth glide,
Challenging all to join their stride.
The frogs leap high in silly ways,
Creating jokes for sunny days.

Finally, the stars peek through,
Giggling at the playful crew.
In this grove of lively cheer,
Every step, joy you'll find near!

Harmonious Breezes in the Shining Orchard

In the orchard, squirrels chatter,
While the birds provoke their patter.
Apples bounce with a little cheer,
As bees dance, buzzing loud and clear.

A goat slips on a patch of grass,
While laughing kids come rushing past.
Lemonade spills, but what a sight!
The ants all march in pure delight.

Under clouds shaped like a hat,
A dog sneezes, chasing a rat.
Trees wiggle with a playful breeze,
Whispering secrets to the leaves.

In chaos, joy is found with ease,
Dancing 'neath the laughing trees.
With every giggle, spirits rise,
In this orchard, laughter flies.

The Radiance of Nature's Cadence

A tortoise rocks in snug retreat,
While rabbits stomp their tiny feet.
Worms wiggle on a dance-off spree,
While frogs support with croaks of glee.

The sunlight shines on every face,
Even ants are in the race.
Tulips sway in the cheeky wind,
As nature plays, we all have sinned.

A butterfly wears polka dots,
And dances near the bubbling pots.
Crickets cheer for the lively scene,
As squirrels juggle with unforeseen.

The branches twist with both delight,
As shadows play from day to night.
Nature's rhythms hum a tune,
Celebrating beneath the moon.

Ethereal Notes from the Verdant Heights

A raccoon strums on a old guitar,
While wise owls contemplate from afar.
Wind chimes giggle with every gust,
Offering notes that shimmer and rust.

The hedgehogs plan a grand parade,
While sunbeams join the lovely charade.
Ducks line dance, an awkward crew,
Chasing shadows, through morning dew.

Toadstools cheer with hats so grand,
As grasshoppers join the band.
Crickets tap with rhythm divine,
The forest floor, a dance floor, fine.

From the heights where laughter swirls,
And nature's melody unfurls,
We join the fun, let's take a chance,
In this symphony, we dance.

The Glowing Heart of the Woodland

In the woodland, giggles are loud,
Even mushrooms wear a plumed shroud.
Foxes prance with a wink and a grin,
While fireflies work their light from within.

The brook sings a bubbly song,
As turtles shuffle along just wrong.
A bear tries to dance with the bees,
Stomping right through the dancing leaves.

Pine trees sway with a gusty cheer,
And woodland creatures gather near.
Chipmunks snicker at a blooper reel,
Where skydiving acorns spin and wheel.

Under stars that laugh and twinkle,
Nature's heart begins to crinkle.
In merriment, we all take part,
In the glowing rhythm of the heart.

Rhythms of the Glittering Trunks

The branches sway, a dance in air,
Squirrels giggle without a care.
The leaves tap their toes, oh so spry,
While shadows bounce, as they pass by.

The trunk gets up, takes a silly spin,
With wobbly roots, it's a best-seller win!
Echoes of laughter from the high-up crew,
Woodpecker beats his drum, it's true!

Symphonies in the Glistening Glade

In the glade where laughter blends,
Frogs croak tunes that never end.
Fireflies flicker, dance in glee,
While the owls hoot jokes, oh whee!

The butterflies spin, swirling bright,
Ticklish breezes take flight at night.
The flowers sway with perky cheer,
As the moonlight grins, drawing near.

Voices of the Luminous Canopy

Whispers of joy float through the leaves,
Chattering chipmunks weave their weaves.
The dazzling light plays peek-a-boo,
As the tree holds secrets, fresh and new.

Up high, the parrots crack a joke,
While the branches sway, the laughter's woke.
The canopy sings in a high-pitched tone,
As critters chuckle, never alone.

Aria of the Shining Foliage

Breezes hum a cheerful refrain,
Dancing leaves sing, joyous and plain.
The branches shake, tickle in time,
While nature's music feels so sublime.

Glimmers and giggles in the light,
With critters prancing, what a sight!
The tree sways gently, a playful tune,
As stars wink back, under the moon.

Songs Amidst the Glistening Grove

In a grove where giggles flow,
Branches dance, and breezes blow.
Squirrels joke and rabbits tease,
Tickling trunks with playful knees.

Raccoons wear hats, oh what a sight,
Mice on stilts, quite the delight.
Leaves rustle in hearty cheer,
Nature's laughter, loud and clear.

Bumblebees sing off-key tunes,
Dancing under glowing moons.
Frogs in tuxedos hop around,
Making mischief, oh what a sound!

A fox plays cards with a wise old owl,
Telling tales that make us howl.
In this glimmering, playful space,
Every creature finds their place.

Incantations of the Vibrant Forest

In a forest where shadows dance,
Woodpeckers jig, and squirrels prance.
Dancing on branches, they all jest,
Creating spells, oh what a fest!

A badger in boots does a jig,
Spinning 'round like a playful twig.
With every step, he shakes the ground,
Echoes of laughter bound and sound.

The leaves whisper secrets and jokes,
As foxes chuckle, winking folks.
Mushrooms giggle, sprouting their heads,
While hedgehogs share tales waking from beds.

A wily raccoon brews tea with flair,
Bouncing about without a care.
In this vibrant, laughing scene,
Every moment feels like a dream.

Melodies Under the Flickering Stars

Under the stars, the critters sing,
Crickets chirp as night takes wing.
Fireflies twinkle like a show,
In this concert, everyone glows.

A cat in pajamas plays guitar,
While raccoons dance, oh how bizarre!
Owls hoot in a rhythmic beat,
Their wise eyes twinkling, oh so sweet.

Bats flip-flop in a dizzy row,
Chasing shadows, stealing the show.
Squirrels clap in the silver light,
Cheering on brightly, what a sight!

The moon grins wide, enjoying the vibe,
While all the creatures unite and jibe.
In this night of sparkling glee,
Their laughter rings forever free.

Serenade of the Resplendent Leaves

Among the leaves, a concert thrives,
Where chipmunks sing and eagles dive.
The foliage shimmers, laughter swells,
As every critter shares their spells.

A raccoon, a chef, with a pot so tall,
Makes soup of sunshine, the best of all.
Mice debate what spice to use,
While ants perform in tiny shoes.

A wise old tree starts telling tales,
Of past adventures, hapless fails.
Its branches sway in giggly fits,
While squirrels marvel at the skits.

With every rustle, a punchline flows,
In the laughter bloom where joy just grows.
In this leafy haven, so brimming with cheer,
Every note plays on, year after year.

Rhythms of the Radiant Roots

In a forest where giggles grow,
The roots play tunes we all know.
They tap and dance with such delight,
Making squirrels laugh all through the night.

The branches sway with silly grace,
As owls join in the funny race.
They hoot and honk, a wacky show,
Under the moon's gleaming glow.

The critters gather, a jolly crew,
Bouncing and bouncing, oh what a view!
Their laughter echoes, a merry sound,
In this magical place, fun is found.

With every rustle, a chuckle is spun,
The forest's party has just begun.
So join the fun and dance around,
In the radiance, joy abounds.

Chants Beneath the Starlit Canopy

Beneath the stars, a quirky choir,
The leaves share jokes that never tire.
With twinkling lights, they serenade,
As fireflies join their giggly parade.

The nightingale struts with flair so bright,
Singing silly songs of pure delight.
While raccoons play a prank or two,
Under the vast sky, their laughter grew.

As shadows dance on the moonlit grass,
The critters gather; they're having a blast.
With chatter and giggles, they lift the gloom,
Making friends beneath the sparkly bloom.

Oh, what a sight under starlit skies,
With laughter bubbling like sweet surprise.
Join the fun; you'll feel so free,
In the night's whimsical jubilee.

Odes to the Bejeweled Bark

On bark so bright, the stories thrive,
Where squirrels scribble and bees dive.
With every swirl, a giggle flows,
In the land where the funny tree grows.

The knots and grains, a comical design,
Each crack revealing a punchline divine.
As chipmunks chuckle and raccoons cheer,
The jewels on the bark bring good vibes near.

A woodpecker drums a silly beat,
Causing the rabbits to dance on their feet.
With each bop and twirl, they join along,
Creating a chorus, a playful song.

In this lively glade, the laughter erupts,
As nature's humor hilariously erupts.
So come take a look and you will see,
Odes sung to the bejeweled glee.

Tunes of the Celestial Foliage

In leaves of green, the laughter soars,
As breezes play like open doors.
The trees hum tunes that tickle the air,
Where squirrels spin stories with flair.

The branches sway, a goofy dance,
Inviting all critters to take a chance.
With wiggles and giggles, they join the fun,
Underneath the warming sun.

The foliage rustles, a ticklish spree,
As the flowers nod to this jubilee.
With bananas and berries, all sorts of treats,
The laughter continues, as joy repeats.

So come one, come all, to the leafy stage,
Where hilarity blooms at every age.
In this garden of giggles, let's all believe,
The tunes of foliage we will achieve.

Harmonies from the Dew-Kissed Branches

The leaves are dancing, such a sight,
Squirrels are twirling, what a delight!
A bird on a branch, a voice like a bell,
Singing of nuts, oh do tell, do tell!

Laughter is dropped like raindrops today,
As rabbits in top hats join in the play.
A frog with a flute joins the merry spree,
Tuning up loud for all to see!

The sun gives a nod, the shadows all prance,
The bees are all buzzing, lost in a trance.
With comical feet and a whimsical leap,
They dance like they've downed an entire heap!

With melodies graced by the ants in a row,
A tiny parade with nowhere to go.
Oh, isn't it strange, how laughter can twine?
A harmony born from the wild and divine!

Whispered Lyrics of the Shimmering Flora

In a meadow where daisies wear hats made of dew,
The grasshoppers giggle as they dance right on cue.
With petals a-flutter, the flowers display,
A dance-off of colors, hip-hip-hooray!

Green beans in sneakers with rhythm so grand,
Join waltzing tomatoes, oh isn't it grand?
The onions are crying, but don't shed a tear,
They're just laughing at carrots who drink too much beer!

Bumblebees buzz it, a silly refrain,
While ladybugs tap dance, showing their gain.
The twilight is painted in tones of pure fun,
Each whisper of wind shares the secrets they've spun!

A bouquet embraces this whimsical spree,
Sprouting enchantments, like glee from a tree.
In laughter and song, nature finds its sweet tune,
Oh the joys that unfold under the glow of the moon!

Ballads in the Jewel-Toned Wilderness

In the wild of the woods where the weird creatures roam,
There's a raccoon in socks, who feels right at home.
With a chorus of owls, they sing with pure glee,
About snacks in the night, oh where could they be?

The fireflies waltz like a disco ball's light,
While wolves on the side start a karaoke night.
With harmonies howling beneath the cool stars,
They all sing of mischief, of cookies and jars!

The goofiest sounds come from rabbits in line,
Who boast of their cabbages, so fresh and so fine.
A moose brings the snacks, with a grin ear to ear,
While chipmunks pass treats, giving every last cheer!

In this jewel-toned wonder, the laughter won't cease,
As critters make music, and everyone's pleased.
The wilderness pulses with joy and delight,
Every creature a singer, under the moonlight!

Echoes of the Glimmering Canopy

Up high in the branches where giggles abound,
The monkeys are swinging, just messing around.
With echoes of laughter, they bounce on the leaves,
Oh, the joy in the trees, nature lightly weaves!

The parrots are chatting with their bright colored tunes,
While butterflies flutter, mimicking balloons.
A fungus in slippers does a silly parade,
As dandelions twirl, their seeds get delayed!

The stream hums along with a bubbly refrain,
While frogs with monocles share knowledge with rain.
The trunks tap their feet, they sway side to side,
In this glimmering grove where the fun cannot hide!

Beneath the bright canopy full of warmth and cheer,
Nature's own laughter is something to hear.
With echoes of joy that linger and spread,
The spirit of play dances over each head!

Whispers of the Dazzling Arbor

Beneath the leaves, a squirrel prances,
With acorns tucked, it takes its chances.
A nutty dance, a quirky waltz,
It laughs aloud, who needs a pulse?

The branches sway, a gentle tease,
The breezy tunes put my mind at ease.
A bird complains, it's out of tune,
While ants move in a grand cartoon.

The flowers giggle, petals wide,
With bees that buzz, they take a ride.
A bumble's bump, a comedy show,
In this bright spot, the laughter flows.

So if you walk beneath this charm,
Grab a seat, soak up the warm.
With every chuckle, nature sings,
In the shimmering trees, oh, the joy it brings!

Odes to the Celestial Glade

In a glade fair, the shadows play,
Where mushrooms dance and squirrels sway.
A rabbit hops, adorned in flair,
Sipping dew like fancy fare.

Sunshine beams and wiggles wide,
While gnomes in hats attempt to hide.
Their little giggles, a clumsy cheer,
Echo all throughout the year.

The daisies chatter, "What's the buzz?"
While crickets croon, "Just because!"
A party here, where tickles thrive,
In a space where we all come alive.

So come and see the merry lot,
In this glade where laughter's caught.
With silly songs and silly sights,
Here every moment simply delights!

Anthems of the Glistening Flora

Amidst the blooms, a snail goes slow,
With every inch, a tale to show.
He wears a shell, a tiny dome,
And calls the garden his funny home.

The flowers sway, they tickle the air,
While butterflies showcase their flair.
A funny twist, a whimsical flight,
In this splashy world, all feels just right.

The wind whispers jokes in playful gusts,
Creating laughter, as nature must.
The petals giggle, and so do we,
In this place of glee, bound and free.

So raise a cheer for flora so bright,
In a wonderland bursting with light.
With every chuckle and every beam,
Nature's antics create the dream!

Lullabies from the Luminous Grove

In the grove, where laughter spills,
A hedgehog plays with twigs and frills.
He rolls around, all stabs and pricks,
A jolly sight that always clicks.

The fireflies blink, a disco ball,
Inviting all to the shimmery hall.
Crickets creak a sleepy tune,
While owls hoot, "We'll sleep by noon!"

The leaves rustle, a gentle sigh,
As whispers blend and dreams float by.
A sleepy bear snores, oh so loud,
While clouds above form a cozy shroud.

So drift along with the giggling breeze,
In this grove, all hearts feel at ease.
With lullabies spun from twinkling light,
Dream a funny dream, till morning bright!

Lullabies from the Lush Greenery

In the garden where giggles grow,
The flowers dance with a silly show.
A daisies' hat, a tulip's shoes,
They prance around spreading silly news.

Squirrels wear ties, oh what a sight!
Bunnies jump in a cozy flight.
They sing to bees with buzzing glee,
"Join our party and dance with me!"

A wobbly vine throws a tart confetti,
While ladybugs twirl all warm and petty.
Each leaf's a stage, each root's a clown,
In this leafy realm, there's never a frown.

So hush now, listen to the fun unfold,
As nature weaves stories, bright and bold.
In the lush, green world where laughter sways,
Lullabies bloom in the silliest ways.

Rhapsody Among the Bursting Blossoms

Petals giggle, colors collide,
Blossoms sway with nothing to hide.
A rose tells jokes to a shy sunflower,
While butterflies flutter with magic power.

A bee named Buzz hosts a dance-off hour,
While daisies declare their quirky flower power.
The peonies stomp with a boisterous cheer,
Even shy violets join in without fear.

Unicorns prance on wobbly stems,
Telling tales of their leafy gems.
An ivy vine makes a comical face,
Chasing down petals in a silly race.

So sing with glee as springtime begins,
With flowers that laugh, let joy spin.
In this vibrant parade where wonders gleam,
The rhapsody flows like a bubbling dream.

Verses in the Sun-Kissed Glade

In the glade where giggles leap,
Sunlight tickles, secrets keep.
A squirrel with shades takes a bold glide,
While flowers gossip, swaying with pride.

Frogs wear crowns of vibrant green,
Croaking tunes, a royal scene.
They ribbit and hop with a cheeky grin,
Inviting all critters to join in the din.

The breeze plays tunes through rustling leaves,
As dragonflies dance, spinning like thieves.
A curious hedgehog joins the snap,
With a tumbly turn, he takes a lap.

So gather round, in this glade so bright,
Where every nook sparks sheer delight.
With verses written by nature's hand,
Let laughter bloom across the land.

Enchantment of the Prismatic Blossoms

Under a rainbow of dizzying hues,
Flowers whisper, oh what fun news!
A zany lilac wears mismatched shoes,
While poppies giggle, sharing their views.

Sunflowers tease with their lofty height,
As pansies wink with sheer delight.
A chubby bumblebee in a flower race,
Buzzes by with a silly, silly face.

Thirty butterflies craft a vivid joke,
While a dandelion splits with a poke.
They pop and twirl, a spectacular flurry,
Sending each petal into a hurry.

So join the fun in this blooming spree,
Where laughter weaves through every tree.
With prismatic blossoms that giggle and sway,
An enchantment blooms, brightening the day.

Rhapsody of the Twinkling Orchard

In the orchard, fruits wear hats,
Singing softly, like chubby cats.
Leaves are dancing, full of glee,
Whispering secrets to the bee.

Apples giggle, pears do prance,
Together they all join the dance.
Sunshine tickles, laughter flows,
While the silly old tree doze.

Branches sway, a wobbly tune,
Underneath a laughing moon.
Squirrels swing from branch to branch,
In this fun, no time to ranch!

Breezy whispers, cherry pies,
Under the cake of sunny skies.
Oh what joy, oh what delight,
In this orchard, hearts take flight.

Dreamscapes Beneath the Shining Trees

Beneath the branches, dreams take flight,
Where butterflies giggle, day and night.
Chubby chipmunks share their tales,
With laughter loud as their tiny wails.

Clouds in pajamas float on by,
While the daisies wink and sigh.
Kittens juggling with the sun,
Makes the afternoons so much fun.

Ladybugs dance in twirly skirts,
Giggling softly, dodging dirt.
Every leaf with a twinkling eye,
Watches dreams pass, flying high.

Boughs that whisper, soft and sweet,
Share the joy of curious feet.
Sing with stars as they prance and play,
In this dreamy, bright ballet.

Enchanted Echoes of the Emerald Haven

In a haven, echoes chatter loud,
Where every flower feels so proud.
Frogs on lily pads start to croon,
In concert with the bright-eyed moon.

Magic giggles in the air,
Twirling leaves without a care.
Dandelions blow their wishes near,
While critters laugh without a fear.

Squirrels wear their fanciest tie,
As they leap and laugh on high.
Nature's circus, wild and free,
An emerald stage for all to see.

Echoes giggle 'neath the trees,
Sharing secrets with the breeze.
In this realm of leafy green,
Playful laughter reigns supreme.

Melodies in the Light-Dappled Meadow

In the meadow, flowers sing,
While butterflies do their fling.
Bumblebees start a merry line,
Wiggling to the sun's sweet shine.

Clouds racing, playing tag up high,
Chasing whispers in the sky.
Frogs in crowns leap with flair,
Joining in the joyful air.

The daisies wear their wackiest hats,
While ants play checkers with their mates.
Every critter joins the fun,
Underneath the warming sun.

With each step, the meadow laughs,
As every shadow jumps and crafts.
Here's a tune, a silly spree,
In this light-dappled jubilee.

Echoes in the Enchanted Forest

Amidst the woods, a squirrel prances,
Chasing thoughts like little glances.
A raccoon dances with a hat,
While birds all giggle at the chat.

Whispers float on breezy jaunts,
Toadstools wear their stylish fonts.
A rabbit juggles carrots high,
As fireflies twinkle in the sky.

Frogs in tuxedos sing a tune,
While critters waltz beneath the moon.
Each leaf claps as the breezes tease,
Join the fun, oh, if you please!

With laughter echoing all around,
The merry creatures share the sound.
When night descends with playful sighs,
Our forest wakes, to all surprise.

Nocturnal Chants of the Verdant Realm

Owl conducts a midnight choir,
While crickets strum their strings of fire.
Mice in capes pirouette and spin,
As shadows join in, let the fun begin!

A badger plays a sax quite grand,
With hedgehogs tapping feet on sand.
The moonbeams wink with cheeky charm,
As nighttime hums a silly psalm.

The stars join in with sparkling glee,
While trees sway gently, sipping tea.
With laughter rising through the air,
The woodland folk shed all their care.

In this realm of mirth and cheer,
The nocturnal songs ring bright and clear.
Beneath the glow, all mischief thrives,
And creatures dance, oh, how they jive!

Rhythmic Reveries of the Glorious Garden

In a garden where the veggies laugh,
Tomatoes giggle, and carrots craft.
Peas do pirouettes, side by side,
While sunflowers beam with joy and pride.

Butterflies chase, all colors bright,
As daisies yawn in morning light.
The pumpkins munch on spicy pie,
And bees buzz tunes that never die.

A beetle rolls a ball of thread,
While marigolds dance, their heads all red.
With every bloom, a laugh is heard,
Nature's chatter in every word.

As rain falls soft, with pitter-pats,
The sprouts do tap-dance, what a chat!
In this glorious, vibrant place,
Every petal shares a silly face!

Harmonies in the dappled sun

In sunlight's glow, the frogs declare,
A symphony beyond compare.
Lily pads are stages bright,
Where nature sings, with pure delight.

The bugs on strings create a show,
As leaflets sway, the breezes blow.
Caterpillars crawl with flair,
This garden stage, who wouldn't dare?

A playful breeze brings giggles near,
While blossoms spread their petals sheer.
Each note they hum, a jolly tune,
That dances sweetly, afternoon.

As shadows play and laughter swirls,
The world engages in its twirls.
With nature's joy, through skies we run,
In dappled light, we laugh and hum!

Hymns from the Vivid Glade

In a glade where giggles reign,
The bushes boast a silly strain.
Frogs dressed in a polka-dot suit,
Dance with joy while chasing fruit.

Squirrels wear hats made of leaves,
And gossip wildly, like bees in eaves.
A rabbit juggles nuts with glee,
While chortles echo, wild and free.

The flowers stretch in a funny way,
Tickled by the breeze at play.
Butterflies strut as if on parade,
Twinkling brightly, they never fade.

Laughter flows from twig to bark,
As fireflies dance, igniting the dark.
In this place where joy is king,
Hymns of happiness take to wing.

Odes of the Glistening Garden

In a garden where the gnomes reside,
With oversized shoes, they glide and slide.
Rabbits wear spectacles, oh so grand,
Sipping tea from a tiny hand.

A tomato sings with a wobble and wiggle,
As beans do the cha-cha with a giggle.
Sunflowers swap their hats with flair,
Competing for laughs, a jovial affair.

The snail holds a concert on a leaf,
While dancing shadows steal the brief.
Fruit flies play tag, oh what a sight,
Creating chaos, pure delight!

In this whimsical, glistening space,
Every corner wears a cheerful face.
Odes of laughter, peace, and cheer,
Ring through the garden, far and near.

Chants of Twilight in the Verdant Realm

In twilight's glow, the crickets croon,
As owls make faces like a cartoon.
Fireflies flicker, jesters they are,
Filling the night with their twinkling star.

A hedgehog rolls in a pizza slice,
While raccoons debate which snack is nice.
The moon winks down with a sly little grin,
As the dancing leaves spin round and spin.

Whispers float from the tip of the grass,
Tales of mischief that never pass.
Each creature chuckles from branch to stump,
Chants of nature, enjoying the jump!

Here in the realm where stories ignite,
Every shadow makes the evening bright.
With laughter ringing through soft, green trails,
Twilight's humor never fails.

Verses of the Radiant Wilderness

In radiant woods where the sun gets shy,
Trees wear sunglasses, oh my, oh my!
Wolves tell jokes with a toothy grin,
While squirrels quip with a cheeky spin.

The brook bubbles up with a hearty laugh,
As beavers engage in a war of craft.
Funky mushrooms have their own band,
Grooving to rhythms of the land.

A lone cactus rattles a quirky tune,
Humming softly, like a crooning moon.
The wildflowers giggle under the sky,
As butterflies flutter and swoop by.

Here in the wilderness, where fun is king,
Every creature revels in the joy they bring.
Verses echo, bright and clear,
Celebrating laughter, year after year.

Echoes from the Twinkling Boughs

In the tree of jolly dreams,
The squirrels dance with gleeful schemes.
They twirl and spin, a fluffy mess,
While chirping birds make quite the fuss.

A parrot wears a tiny hat,
He thinks he's cool, yet he's just fat.
He sings off-key, but that's okay,
In this wild tree, we laugh and play.

The raccoons throw a wild surprise,
With acorn pies, they aim for skies.
Missed their mark, the pies did splat,
Cream-filled chaos, what's funnier than that?

The sun beams down, the laughter swells,
Echoes ring in these leafy bells.
A dancing gnome, with shoes so bright,
Unites the grove in pure delight.

Harmonies of the Luminous Leaves

The leaves shimmer in a breezy sway,
They whisper jokes in a leafy play.
One thinks it's wise, a sage indeed,
But turns out it's just a clumsy seed.

Crickets join in, playing their tune,
Dancing round the glow of the moon.
They trip and fall on wooden logs,
Chasing after their own lost frogs.

A raccoon sings with lips so dry,
He forgot the words, oh my, oh my!
The fireflies flicker, all aglow,
They light the stage for this funny show!

Amidst the giggles, the trees delight,
In harmonious laughter, they shine so bright.
With every rustle, another jest,
Nature's comedy is simply the best.

Ballad of the Dazzling Branches

Branches gleam with sparkle and flair,
While playful critters dance in the air.
A beaver spins tales with sticks and twine,
His log cabin dreams, oh how they shine!

The owls hoot jokes in the cool night,
While fireflies twinkle, oh what a sight!
They drift and dive like little stars,
Laughing at dreams of time on Mars.

The branches sway with giggles and hums,
As each critter jumps and thuds with 'thumps'.
A boisterous laugh from a shy little mouse,
As he tumbles down his leafy house.

With dreamy sounds and crazy cheers,
The dazzling branches have no fears.
Laughter echoes through the twilight,
In this whimsical world, all feels right.

Serenade of the Glittering Orchard

In the orchard where the fruits grin wide,
Each apple chuckles, bursting with pride.
Bouncing berries join the fun,
They play tag until the day is done.

The moonbeams bounce, the shadows prance,
As bunnies gather for a moonlit dance.
A clumsy hare trips on a vine,
He laughs it off with a cheeky whine.

The frogs serenade with croaks and flops,
While dizzy bees do perfect hops.
They slip and slide on dew-kissed ground,
In a sparkling orchard where joy is found.

So raise a toast with apples piled high,
In this glittering realm, we laugh and sigh.
Together we sing, together we cheer,
In this lively orchard, forever dear.

Enchanted Melodies of the Verdant Canopy

In the leafy dance of spring's delight,
A squirrel sings off-key with all its might.
The flowers giggle at the worm's ballet,
While bees play hopscotch, buzzing all the way.

Underneath the boughs, we loved to sway,
With birds composing tunes that disarray.
A chubby rabbit joins the merry tune,
And sings of carrots beneath the bright moon.

The branches wiggle like they have a tick,
Laden with secrets and a few good tricks.
When night falls down, the star crickets play,
While owls hoot jokes about the day's fray.

In this funny grove, laughter is the key,
Where every creature hops up with glee.
So take a seat and join the hilarious spree,
In the lunacy of the verdant canopy.

Timeless Echoes in the Shimmering Thicket

A frog in a tuxedo croaks a fine tune,
While fireflies dance with lights that swoon.
The grass tickles toes and we burst into fits,
As a fox tells tales that are full of wits.

Beneath the bushes, a party unfolds,
As the hedgehogs share their stories bold.
The tree trunk shakes with each hearty laugh,
While turtles offer logical paths to the staff.

The raccoon in shades is the DJ tonight,
Spinning fun beats beneath the pale light.
And as shadows twirl in the moon's embrace,
Every critter grins in this whimsical place.

So raise a leaf cup to our stars so bright,
For merry echoes fill the cool night.
Together we laugh till the sun breaks free,
In the timeless thicket of jubilee.

Whispers of the Glimmering Grove

A cat on a branch whispers silly trends,
While mice roll around and tap their best bends.
The daisies gossip about the butterfly,
Who wears polka dots and can surely fly.

Chipmunks in dance form a conga line,
While whispers of joy are spun by the vine.
A kookaburra cracks jokes on a whim,
And the woodland creatures all laugh at him.

As leaves rustle gently, secrets unfurl,
While twilight drapes its magical swirl.
Each twig strums a note, a playful tease,
Inviting us all to sway with the breeze.

In this glimmering grove where fun never ends,
Every shadow is grinning, even the bends.
With whispers and giggles, let's dance and sing,
In the cheery embrace of the joy that we bring.

Melodies of the Shimmering Canopy

A parrot wears shades, crooning with flair,
As the blossoms share secrets, a comical air.
With crickets as drummers, they set the beat,
While a sloth takes a nap, missing the heat.

The trees sway side to side, a funny march,
As squirrels throw acorns, making a parch.
A hedgehog tells tales of dandelion dreams,
While the sun giggles bright, bursting at the seams.

Each critter involved in this playful scheme,
Creating a symphony that feels like a dream.
The frogs join in chorus, full of delight,
As a playful sunbeam brings laughter to light.

So join this parade in the canopy high,
Where every leaf twirls and spirits can fly.
With melodies echoing through branches so free,
Let's shake up the grove with our joyful spree.

Melody in the Jewel-Toned Glade

In a glade where colors dance,
The squirrels put on funny pants.
They twirl around with great delight,
Stealing acorns left and right.

A bird in shades of bright magenta,
Sings to frogs in a grand crescendo.
The frogs reply with croaks and cheer,
"More nuts, more tunes, let's persevere!"

A bunny hops with style and grace,
Wearing sunglasses, keeping pace.
With every leap, the colors sway,
The glade's a circus come what may.

The trees join in with rustling leaves,
As laughter bounces, joy believes.
In Nature's patch, a crafted spree,
Where silly hearts roam wild and free.

Musings of the Radiating Orchard

In an orchard bright with glowing fruit,
The apples joke, "Don't be a brute!"
They spin around with cheeky pride,
While pears giggle, trying to hide.

A wily fox with boots of red,
Tries to dance but trips instead.
The fruits all laugh, their glee a song,
In this orchard where no one's wrong.

A wise old owl gives a stern look,
Says, "Silly fruits, you're off the hook!"
With puns and jests flying like kites,
The laughter echoes through the nights.

A dance-off starts, fruits in a row,
Bouncing colors put on a show.
With every twist, the giggles grow,
In this orchard, joy's the way we flow.

Rhapsody Under the Glimmering Stars

Beneath the stars so big and bright,
A raccoon wears a hat, what a sight!
He strums a tune on a silver tin,
While owls hoot, "Let the party begin!"

Fireflies flicker, dancing like mad,
Chasing shadows, making the night glad.
One tripped up, fell right on a leaf,
And giggles spread like wild disbelief.

A hedgehog rolls with tumbling cheer,
Shouting, "Hey, I'm a shooting star here!"
The critters clap to the rhythm they find,
Under sparkle and giggles, all intertwined.

As moonbeams glint on the merry scene,
A troupe of raccoons asks, "Where's the cuisine?"
Laughter rings out, a whimsical cheer,
Under stars that twinkle, so bright and near.

Whispers of the Ethereal Grove

In a grove where shadows giggle low,
Mice in pajamas put on a show.
They quickstep past with tiny delight,
Making sure everyone's out of sight.

The trees shake hands, their branches sway,
With zealous whispers, they join the play.
"Who's got the cookies?" they ask in a hush,
As the sun gleams bright in a morning rush.

A rabbit sportin' a silly hat,
Chimes in with a little chat.
He pulls out tricks, all silly and sweet,
"Let's start a dance, everyone on your feet!"

Fairies flitter with laughter anew,
Sprinkling joy like morning dew.
In this grove, where magic's alive,
Every moment's a jolly jive.

Duets of the Vibrant Flora

In the garden where daisies chatter,
Tulips gossip about the weather.
A gnome in a hat with a very tall crown,
Tries to juggle, but falls right down!

Bees buzz tunes in a busy choir,
While butterflies dance, soaring higher.
A squirrel with shades on the branch overhead,
Sips acorn tea while the whole world's fed!

With laughter and blooms, it's a sight to see,
The petals are giggling, oh, the jubilee!
While the roses tell jokes, oh what a tease!
Even the bumblebees laugh with ease!

In this patch of delight, chaos ensues,
As daisies retell the stories they choose.
So gather around, let the mirth take a swing,
For nature's a stage, always ready to fling!

Lyrical Dance of the Silvery Branches

The willow sways with a comical twist,
Making birdies shake their wings in a mist.
While the oak tree chuckles at passing ants,
Who can't find their way, doing little dance prance!

A raccoon in slippers sneaks closer to peek,
At squirrels debating who's tops in hide-and-seek!
Branches giggle, sharing secrets grown,
While dappled light sparkles, setting the tone!

With branches that 'sway' to a whimsical tune,
The forest feels like a morning cartoon!
Frogs croak out symphonies filled with delight,
As owls roll their eyes at the bright shining light!

Oh, laughter rings out in the rustling leaves,
Creating a movement that never deceives.
Just join this jig where the trees are the stars,
And dance with delight under moonlight bazars!

Serenade of the Dappled Light

In patches of sun where shadows play tricks,
The light sings sweet songs, a comical mix.
A deer struts by with a flair for the grand,
While a chipmunk asks, 'Do you lend a helping hand?'

Frogs croak like singers on the big stage,
With bullfrogs proclaiming their green, croaky rage.
The firs sway and laugh in the soft, gentle breeze,
Whispering tales that can bring you to knees!

And up in the branches, the owls they jest,
With hoots like applause, who's the very best?
The sunlight's a jester, tickling the ground,
As giggles from moss and the wind dance around!

So gather 'round folks, in this lively glen,
Let merriment sprout like the roots from a pen.
For light here is laughter, a joyful ballet,
As nature composes a bright, funny play!

Verses in the Jewel-Studded Forest

In the forest where diamonds are scattered on leaves,
A squirrel wears bling, and he proudly believes.
The rabbits all sing, clad in sequined attire,
While the trees cheer them on—do they twirl? Oh, dire!

Jewel beetles boast in their shimmer and shine,
While the fawns sip spring with a taste—so divine!
A parrot recites in a voice rich and bold,
Telling tall tales of treasures untold!

A fox with a top hat sells magic in twirls,
As laughter erupts, bringing joy to the girls.
The gems light their eyes as they prance and they glide,
Creating a thrill, a glittery ride!

In this wonderful world, where humor is gold,
Each critter's an actor, being clever and bold.
So dance with the sparkles that shimmer and sway,
In a jubilee forest that's always at play!

Anthems of the Shining Wilderness

In the woods where squirrels dance,
A party starts with a lively chance.
The owls hoot out of tune,
While raccoons strut like they're in a cartoon.

The trees sway, a comedic show,
With branches flailing to and fro.
Bunnies bounce, they're quite the crowd,
While the frogs croak, feeling proud.

A bear comes in with a big old grin,
Sipping honey, let the laughter begin!
Nature's jokesters, a humorous mix,
In this wilderness, we find our kicks.

As the sun sets, the shadows play,
Crickets chirp in a funny way.
With every giggle, the forest sings,
In this wild world, joy's what it brings.

Enchanted Whispers of the Luminous Glen

In a glen where the lights do twinkle,
The frogs hold court, their voices sprinkle.
A firefly jokes, but nobody gets,
What the glowbug means with his funny threats.

The hedgehogs roll in the dewy grass,
Chasing each other, oh what a class!
With prickles out, they race about,
Their laughter rings, no hint of doubt.

A wise old owl, perched on a pine,
Tells tales of owls, all mix and shine.
In this glen, the laughter flows,
With each chuckle, the humor grows.

As twilight falls, the stars come out,
A symphony of giggles is what it's about.
Among the whispers and the light,
The glen's a stage, pure delight.

Harmonies of the Star-Kissed Realm

In the realm where stars do wink,
A goat sings silly, on the brink.
His voice like gravel, a tune to behold,
Leaves all critters giggling, uncontrolled.

A raccoon plays the saxophone,
Making sweet sounds, all on his own.
But the cat tries to steal the show,
With a meow-theory, but it's a no-go!

The sky is a canvas for mischief and cheer,
The chattering creatures all gathered near.
With comet tails like ribbons of fun,
In this cosmic jam, the laughter won.

As meteors whoosh, they light the night,
Dancing dreams take off in flight.
In this star-kissed space, joy spreads wide,
With every note, the cosmos is our ride.

Ballad of the Shimmering Glades

In shimmering glades where shadows play,
Lively critters gather, night and day.
A fox struts with a swagger so sly,
Cracking jokes that are hard to deny.

The deer prance in with a side-step twirl,
Each leap a dance, giving a whirl.
The hares hop in with a swift, bold cheer,
And crack up the crowd with their funny leer.

As the moon climbs high, the laughter swells,
The glowworms gossip, they have their tales.
In a world of shimmer, the silliness shines,
Lighting up hearts like vintage wines.

With twinkling eyes and joyous grins,
The glades come alive, as happiness spins.
In these woods, where comedy's grand,
Together we laugh, hand in hand.